Guitar

Scottish Folk Tunes for Guitar

31 Traditional Pieces Arranged for Guitar

Edited by / Edition de / Herausgegeben von

Hugh Burns

With accompanying CD
Avec disque compact
Mit Begleit-CD

ED 13359
ISMN M-2201-3221-6
ISBN 978-1-84761-239-7

D1262106

Mid-Continent Public Library
15616 East US Highway 24
Independence, MO 64050

www.schott-music.com

Mainz · London · Berlin · Madrid · New York · Paris · Prague · Tokyo · Toronto

Acknowledgements

Thank you to the following people for their help in preparing this book; text preparation Gaspar Gonzalez; recording Roy Dodds; music copyist Duncan Schmoll; for his support and inspiration Daisaka Ikeda.

Remerciements

Un grand merci aux personnes suivantes pour leur aide dans la préparation de ce recueil : préparation de la partition Gaspar Gonzalez ; enregistrement Roy Dodds ; copiste Duncan Schmoll ; pour son encouragement et son inspiration Daisaka Ikeda.

Danke

Ich danke folgenden Personen für ihre Hilfe bei der Entstehung dieses Buches: Gaspar Gonzalez für die Textbearbeitung, Roy Dodds für die Aufnahme und Duncan Schmoll für die Notenherstellung; Daisaka Ikeda für seine Ermutigung und Inspiration.

ED 13359
British Library Cataloguing-in-Publication Data.
A catalogue record for this book is available from the British Library

ISMN M-2201-3221-6
ISBN 978-1-84761-239-7

© 2011 Schott Music Ltd, London

Recorded at Living Room Studios
Guitars used in recording: Martin D35, Collings (hi-strung), Vintage (low-strung),
Roger Dean, Pedro Maldonado
Guitar set-up: Mike Cameron

French translation: Michaëla Rubi
German translation: Heike Brühl
Design and typesetting by www.adamhaystudio.com
Music setting and page layout by Bev Wilson
Cover photography: iStockphoto.com
Printed in Germany S&Co.8715

Contents/ Sommaire/ Inhalt

The Pieces/ Les morceaux/ Die Stücke

Slow Airs – Songs/ Chansons/ Lieder
Logie o' Buchan
The Bonnie Lass o' Bon Accord
The Spinning Wheel
MacPherson's Lament
The Road and the Miles to Dundee
The Warrior of Persie
A Fond Farewell

Strathspeys
Cawdor Fair
The Keel Row
Orange and Blue
The Braes o' Mar
Highland Whiskey

Reels
The De'il Among the Tailors
The Mason's Apron
The Soldier's Joy
The Merry Blacksmith
Mrs McLeod
My Love She's But a Lassie Yet
Dashing White Sergeant

Jigs
The Piper o' Dundee
Haste to the Wedding
Nan Clark's Jig
Garry Owen
Slip Jig

Waltzes
Will ye Gang to Kelvin Grove
The Rowan Tree
Ye Banks and Braes

Introduction

Scottish traditional music is popular in many countries throughout the world and has influenced many other forms of music including Country and Bluegrass. Many Scottish and Irish traditional musicians avoid the term Celtic music, which is often used to describe styles, which can range from harp melodies to the Jigs and Reels of country-dance music. The use of the term Celtic music, whether it is correct or not, has helped to promote a wide interest in older folk songs and traditional melodies.

The book contains a wide selection of traditional songs, pipe and fiddle tunes and a few original pieces arranged for plectrum and finger-style guitar. The tunes can be played solo, with a 2nd guitarist or in a group session.

If you are unfamiliar with the melodies in this book, start by playing the accompanying CD; listen to the music until you can whistle or sing along with the tunes. This will help to develop your ear for Scottish and Celtic music.

Next look at the music and tab and decide the best fingering. I have made a number of suggestions, which work well for most people. However, feel free to experiment with different ideas.

The key is to learn the tunes. Try to play the piece from the beginning to the end, paying careful attention to the rhythm. If this is too difficult, break the tune down into 2 or 4 bar phrases and practise them at a slower tempo.

It is important to listen to recordings by great artists (see list p. 57) as this will help you develop a better feeling for the music.

Scottish music has always been strongly connected with society, for example dances, social gatherings, weddings, wakes and funerals. Music for a purpose; to enjoy, to inspire and to console like Niel Gow's 'Lament for the death of his wife'. Understanding the different types of dance forms is crucial if you want to learn Scottish music. The rhythm is everything if the music is being played for dance. In solo playing the stylistic ornaments become vital to bring out the richness and detail of the music. Often it is the use of ornaments, vibrato, slides, hammer-on and pull-off techniques, which define the individual player's style.

The basic tune can be interpreted in many ways according to the context in which it is being performed. If the music is played for dance there are strict conventions within the tradition about how the 'set' is put together. Tunes are often in 4 or 8 bar sections with an A and B part. It is common to repeat both parts 2 or 3 times. The tunes can then be segued together to complete the form of the dance.

In Scottish dances a 'set' of 3 Reels are often played together or sometimes a slower Strathspey can lead to a faster Reel.

The Instruments

The Highland bagpipe is the instrument most people associate with Scottish music and it has played a vital role in the development of the many aspects including special ornaments and drones, which have become synonymous with the style.

Gaelic singing and harp playing probably pre-date the bagpipes as many of the pipe ornaments are said to imitate the intonation of the Gaelic language. In the 17th and 18th century many printed collections of Scots songs were published. The Scots Musical Museum, published between 1787 and 1803, included some contributions by Robert Burns.

The vocal music often in the form of Ballads could be sung a cappella or with fiddle, harp or more recently with accordion or guitar accompaniment. The guitar is wonderful for playing this type of music as you can create drones or harmony and have the ability to create ornaments similar to the violin, bagpipe or voice.

Aural Tradition

The repertoire is constantly being re-interpreted as each new generation of musicians add their particular voice to the tradition, in this way the music is always developing.

Dance Styles

The Reel, Hornpipe, Strathspey and Jig all come from the Scottish country-dance tradition. Most Highland or Scottish Reels are performed in 2/4 and 4/4 times, and can often be written in a cut common time signature.

The Strathspey has a distinctive rhythmic pattern known as the Scottish snap. This is also found in the Schottische. The Strathspey can be played at slow or medium tempos. The word Hornpipe refers to a type of reed pipe. It is also the name of a step or 'tap' dance. Jigs are written in 6/8 and 9/8 times. The 9/8 is more common in Ireland where it is known as the 'Slip Jig.'

Introduction

La musique traditionnelle écossaise est populaire dans beaucoup de pays du monde et a influencé nombre d'autres genres musicaux, en particulier la country et le bluegrass. Les musiciens traditionnels écossais et irlandais évitent souvent le terme de musique celtique couramment utilisé pour décrire des styles aussi différents que les mélodies pour harpe ou les musiques de danses populaires telles que jigs et reels. Cependant, l'emploi du terme de musique celtique, qu'il soit approprié ou non, a permis de susciter un vaste intérêt pour les chansons folkloriques anciennes et pour les mélodies traditionnelles.

Ce recueil propose un large choix de chansons traditionnelles, d'airs de cornemuse et de violon ainsi que quelques pièces originales arrangées pour la guitare, avec ou sans utilisation du plectre. Les airs peuvent être joués en solo ou avec un second guitariste ainsi que lors de sessions de groupe.

Si les mélodies de ce recueil ne vous sont pas familières, commencez par écouter le CD d'accompagnement et vous imprégner de la musique jusqu'à ce que vous soyez en mesure de siffler ou de chanter les airs. Vous développerez ainsi votre sens de la musique écossaise et celtique.

Ensuite, regardez la partition et les tablatures et décidez du meilleur doigté. J'ai fait un certain nombre de suggestions qui fonctionnent bien pour la plupart des gens. Cependant, sentez-vous libres d'expérimenter d'autres idées.

La clé de cette musique réside dans la connaissance et l'apprentissage des airs. Essayez de jouer chaque pièce du début à la fin en faisant bien attention au rythme. Si cela vous paraît trop difficile, découpez l'air en phrases de 2 ou 4 mesures et travaillez-les à un tempo plus lent.

Il est important d'écouter les enregistrements de grands musiciens (voir liste p. 59), afin de développer un meilleur sens pour cette musique.

La musique écossaise a toujours été étroitement liée aux événements de la vie sociale : bals, réunions entre amis, mariages, veillées, funérailles etc. Musique fonctionnelle, musique pour le plaisir, l'inspiration ou la consolation, comme le *Lament for the death of his wife* – Lamento pour la mort de sa femme, de Niel Gow. Comprendre les différents types de formes de danses est crucial si vous voulez apprendre la musique écossaise. S'agissant de musique à danser, le rythme est primordial. Lorsque l'on joue en solo, les ornements stylistiques prennent une importance vitale, car ils permettent de faire ressortir la richesse et les subtilités de cette musique. L'ornementation, l'utilisation du vibrato, du *slide* (glissé) et des techniques de *hammer-on* (lié ascendant) ou de *pull-off* (lié descendant) sont d'ailleurs les éléments qui définissent le style individuel de chaque musicien.

Un air de base peut être interprété de nombreuses manières selon le contexte dans lequel il est joué. Si la musique est destinée à être dansée, la tradition impose des conventions strictes quant à la construction d'un « set ». Les airs comprennent en général des phrases de 4 ou 8 mesures, avec une partie A et une partie B. Ces deux parties sont couramment répétées deux à trois fois. Les airs peuvent ensuite être enchaînés pour parachever la forme de danse.

Un « set » de danses écossaises comprend souvent trois *reels*. Il peut aussi arriver qu'un strathspey assez lent débouche sur un reel plus rapide.

Les instruments

La cornemuse des Highlands est l'instrument que la plupart des gens associent à la musique écossaise. Elle a joué un rôle primordial dans le développement de nombreux éléments musicaux, y compris des ornements spécifiques et des bourdons qui sont devenus synonymes de ce style.

Le chant et la harpe gaéliques sont vraisemblablement antérieurs à la cornemuse dans la mesure où de nombreux ornements de la cornemuse sont réputés imiter l'intonation de la langue gaélique. Le 17e et le 18e siècle ont vu la publication d'un grand nombre de recueils de chansons écossaises. Le *Scots Musical Museum*, publié entre 1787 et 1803, incluait notamment des contributions de Robert Burns.

Se présentant souvent sous la forme de ballades, la musique vocale pouvait être chantée *a cappella* ou avec un accompagnement de violon, de harpe ou plus récemment, d'accordéon ou de guitare. La guitare est un instrument merveilleux pour ce type de musique, car elle permet de créer des bourdons ou des harmonies ainsi que des ornements similaires à ceux du violon, de la cornemuse ou de la voix.

Tradition orale

Le répertoire est constamment réinterprété, chaque nouvelle génération de musiciens ajoutant sa voix personnelle à la tradition. En ce sens, cette musique n'a jamais cessé de se développer.

Styles de danses

Reel, hornpipe, strathspey et jig sont toutes des danses issues de la tradition des danses populaires écossaises. La plupart des reels des Highlands ou écossais sont joués à 2/4 ou à 4/4 et sont fréquemment écrits en 2/2.

Le strathspey présente un motif rythmique spécifique connu sous le nom de *Scottish snap* que l'on trouve également dans l'écossaise. Cette danse se joue à un tempo lent à intermédiaire. Le terme de hornpipe fait référence à un certain type de tuyau à anche. Il désigne également une danse pratiquée avec des claquettes. Les jigs sont écrites en 6/8 et en 9/8. La jig en 9/8 est plus courante en Irlande où on l'appelle *slip jig* – gigue glissée.

Einleitung

Traditionelle schottische Musik ist in vielen Ländern auf der ganzen Welt beliebt und hat zahlreiche andere Musikformen beeinflusst, u.a. Country und Bluegrass. Viele schottische und irische Folk-Musiker vermeiden den Begriff keltische Musik, der oft für Stilrichtungen verwendet wird, die von den Harfenstücken bis zu den Jigs und Reels der Country-Dance-Musik reicht. Der Begriff keltische Musik, ob korrekt oder nicht, hat erheblich zur Entstehung eines großen Interesses an älteren Folksongs und traditionellen Melodien beigetragen

Das Buch enthält eine große Auswahl an Volksliedern, Dudelsack- und Fiddle-Tunes sowie ein paar Originalstücke für Plektrum und Fingerstyle-Gitarre. Die Stücke können solo, mit einem zweiten Gitarristen oder in einer Gruppe gespielt werden.

Wenn du die Stücke im Buch nicht kennst, hörst du dir am besten zuerst die Begleit-CD an, bis du die Stücke mitsingen oder -pfeifen kannst. Dadurch bekommst du einen besseren Zugang zur schottischen bzw. keltischen Musik.

Als Nächstes schaust du dir die Noten und Tabulatur an und entscheidest dich für den besten Fingersatz. Ich habe zahlreiche Vorschläge gemacht, mit denen die meisten Gitarristen gut zurechtkommen. Allerdings kannst du natürlich gerne auch andere Ideen ausprobieren.

Das Wichtigste ist, die Stücke zu lernen. Du kannst probieren, sie von Anfang bis Ende durchzuspielen, wobei du genau auf den Rhythmus achten solltest. Wenn das zu schwierig ist, kannst du das Stück in zwei- oder viertaktige Phrasen unterteilen und diese langsamer üben.

Es ist ausgesprochen hilfreich, Aufnahmen bedeutender Künstler (s. Liste s. 62) zu hören, um ein besseres Gefühl für die Musik zu bekommen.

Schottische Musik war schon immer eng mit dem gesellschaftlichen Leben verbunden, z.B. mit Tanzveranstaltungen, Zusammenkünften, Hochzeiten, Totenwachen oder Beerdigungen. Die Musik diente häufig einem bestimmten Zweck: Vergnügen, Inspiration oder auch Trost, wie z.B. Niel Gows „Lament for the death of his wife." Es ist wichtig, die verschiedenen Tanzformen zu verstehen, wenn man schottische Musik spielen möchte – und der Rhythmus ist das Allerwichtigste , wenn die Musik als Tanzbegleitung gespielt wird. Beim Solospiel sind die stilistischen Verzierungen wichtig, um die Vielfältigkeit und Details der Musik hervorzuheben. Oft wird der Stil eines Gitarristen durch seine Verwendung von Verzierungen wie Vibrato, Slide (Glissando), Hammer-on und Pull-off definiert.

Ein Stück kann auf vielfältige Weise interpretiert werden – je nach Kontext, in dem es gespielt wird. Wenn die Musik als Tanzbegleitung gespielt wird, gibt es strenge Konventionen, wie ein „Set" zusammenzustellen ist. Die Stücke bestehen oft aus vier- oder achttaktigen Abschnitten mit einem A- und B-Teil. Es ist üblich, beide Teile zwei- oder dreimal zu wiederholen. Dann können die Stücke ineinander übergeleitet werden.

In schottischen Tänzen wird häufig ein „Set" aus drei Reels gespielt, manchmal auch ein langsamerer Strathspey als Übergang zu einem schnelleren Reel.

Die Instrumente

Der Dudelsack ist das Instrument, das die meisten Menschen mit schottischer Musik assoziieren. Er spielte eine führende Rolle in der Entwicklung der zahlreichen typischen Aspekte dieser Musik, u.a. spezieller Verzierungen und Borduntöne.

Die gälische Vokal- und Harfenmusik ist wahrscheinlich älter als der Dudelsack, da viele Dudelsackverzierungen vermutlich die Intonation der gälischen Sprache imitieren. Im 17. und 18. Jahrhundert wurden viele schottische Liedersammlungen publiziert. Das „Scots Musical Museum" wurde zwischen 1787 und 1803 veröffentlicht und enthielt einige Beiträge von Robert Burns.

Vokalmusik bestand häufig aus Balladen und wurde a cappella oder mit Geigen- oder Harfenbegleitung, in jüngerer Zeit auch mit Akkordeon- oder Gitarrenbegleitung gesungen. Die Gitarre ist hervorragend für diese Musikrichtung geeignet, da man Borduntöne bzw. Harmonien spielen und wie mit der Geige, dem Dudelsack oder der menschlichen Stimme Verzierungen erzeugen kann.

Mündliche Überlieferung

Das Repertoire wird ständig neu interpretiert, da jede neue Musikergeneration die Tradition auf ihre eigene Art und Weise prägt, so dass sich die Musik immer weiterentwickelt.

Tanzformen

Reel, Hornpipe, Strathspey und Jig haben ihren Ursprung in der schottischen Country-Dance-Tradition. Die meisten Highland oder schottischen Reels stehen im 2/4- und 4/4-Takt und können oft alla breve notiert werden.

Der Strathspey hat einen unverkennbaren Rhythmus, der als „Scottish Snap" bezeichnet wird und auch im Schottisch vorkommt. Er kann langsam oder mittelschnell gespielt werden. Das Wort Hornpipe bezieht sich auf ein historisches Rohrblattinstrument, aber auch auf einen Stepptanz. Jigs stehen im 6/8- und 9/8-Takt. Der 9/8-Takt kommt häufiger in Irland vor, wo er als „Slip Jig" bekannt ist.

1. The De'il Among the Tailors

Trad. arr. Hugh Burns

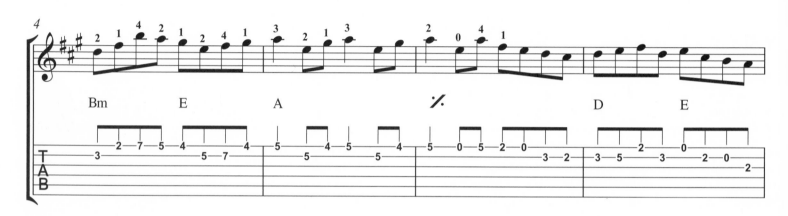

After 2nd repeat
D.S. al Fine

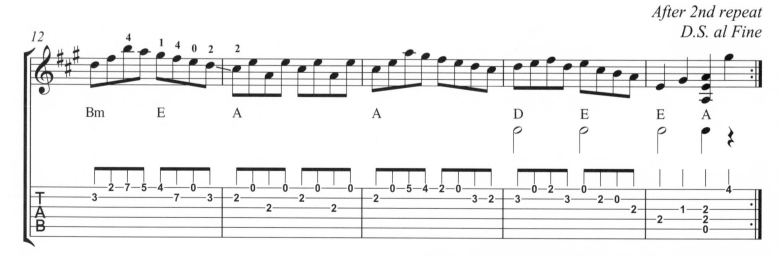

2. The Soldier's Joy

Trad. arr. Hugh Burns

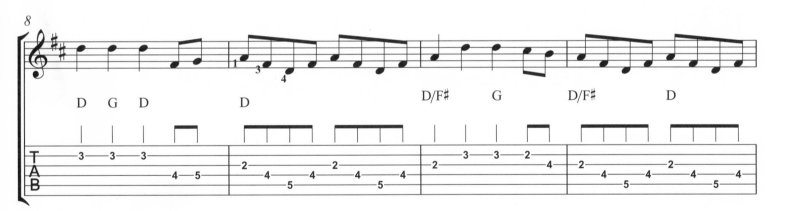

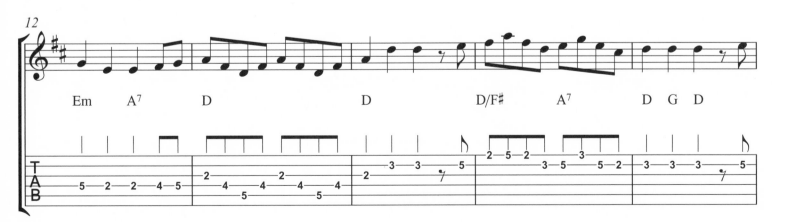

10

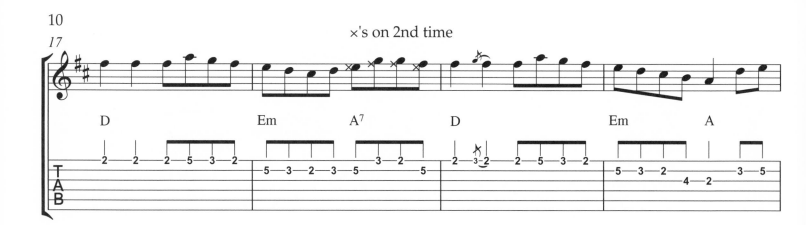

×'s on 2nd time

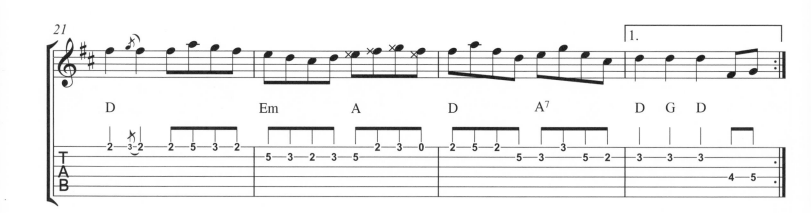

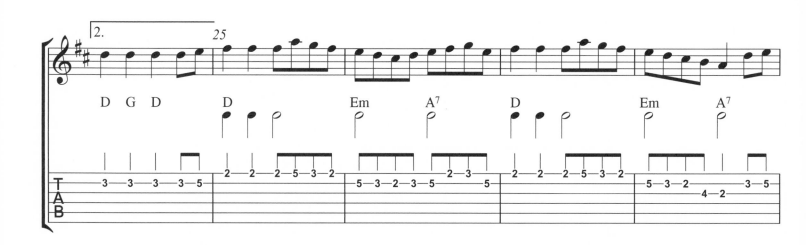

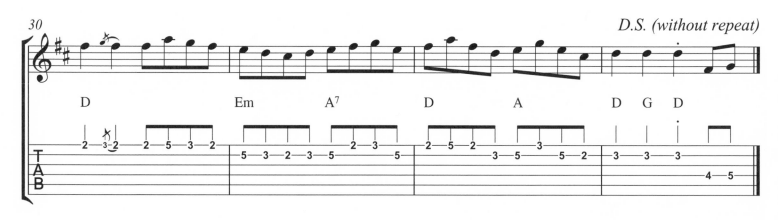

D.S. (without repeat)

End

D   G   D

3. The Mason's Apron

Trad. arr. Hugh Burns

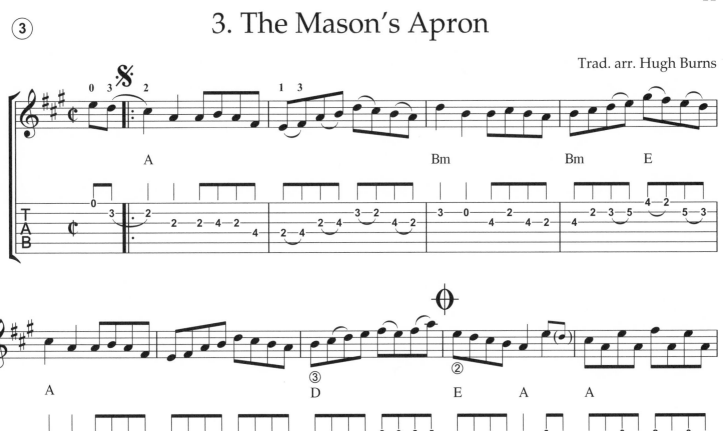

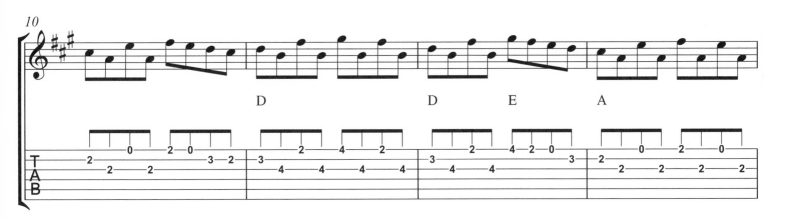

After 2nd repeat
D.S. al Coda

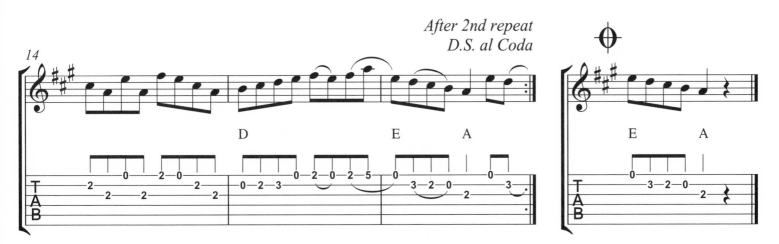

4. The Merry Blacksmith

Trad. arr. Hugh Burns

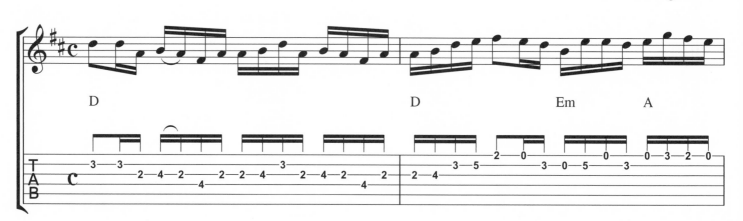

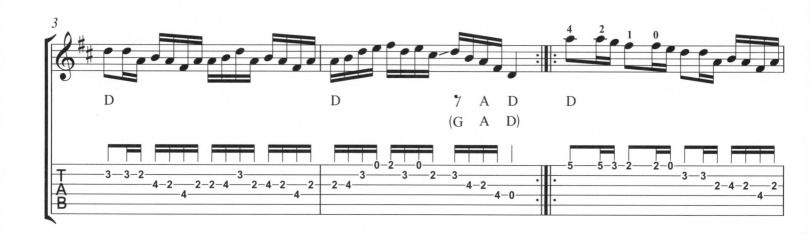

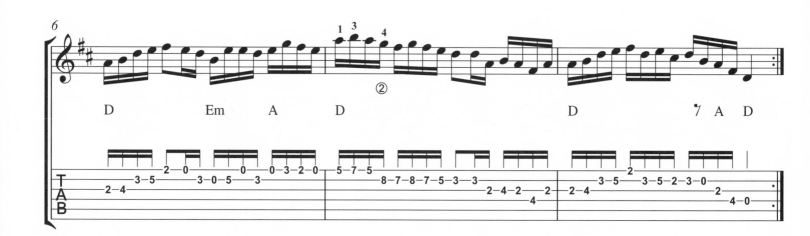

5. Mrs MacLeod

Trad. arr. Hugh Burns

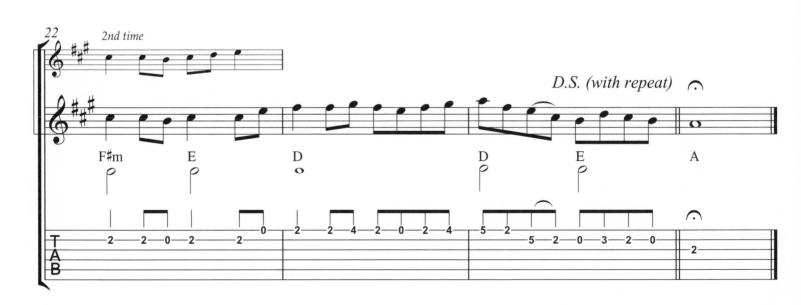

6. The Piper o' Dundee

Capo IV

Trad. arr. Hugh Burns

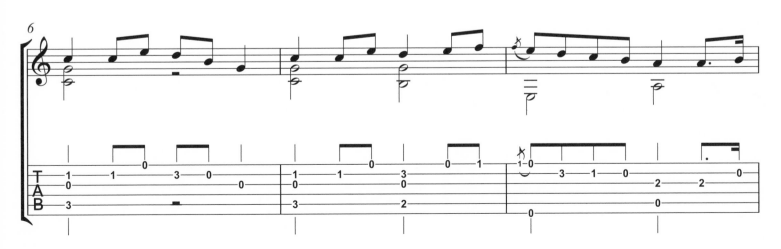

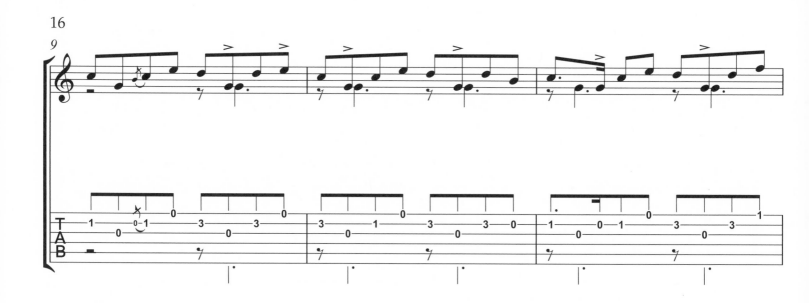

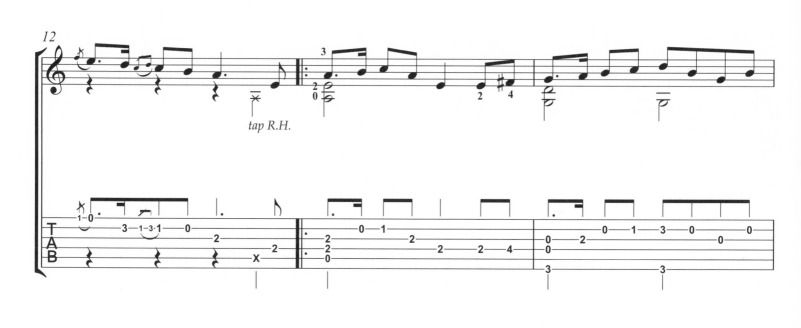

7. Logie o' Buchan

Play tune freely with the feeling of a slow Air. The 'G' tuning gives a special quality, play legato and bring out all the harmony, leaving the notes to ring out.

Trad. arr. Hugh Burns

⑥ = D
⑤ = G

18

8. The Bonnie Lass o' Bon Accord

Trad. arr. Hugh Burns

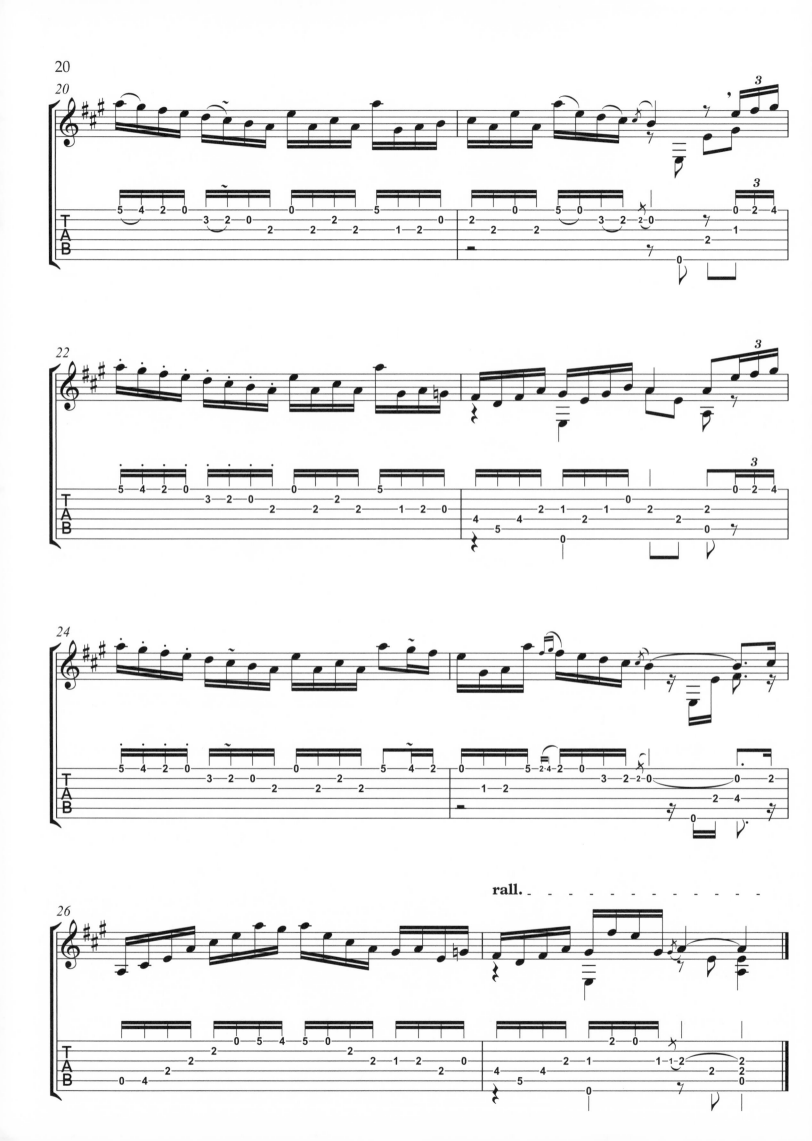

9. The Spinning Wheel

Trad. arr. Hugh Burns

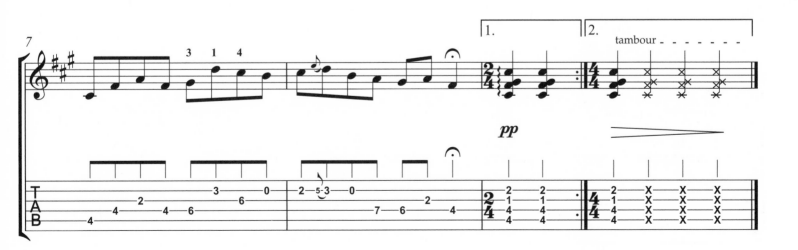

10. MacPherson's Lament

Trad. arr. Hugh Burns

Capo II

Play with feeling

(11)

11. My Love She's But a Lassie Yet

Trad. arr. Hugh Burns

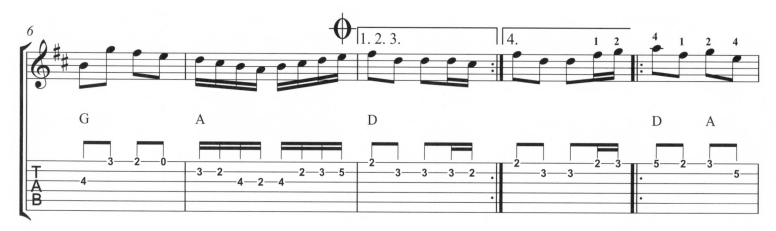

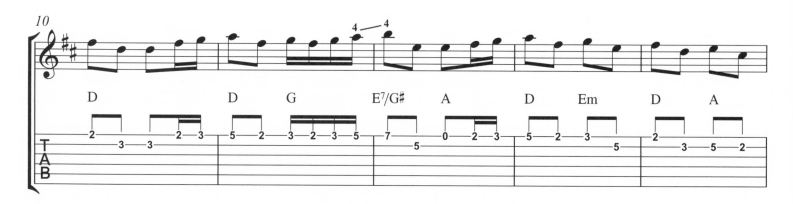

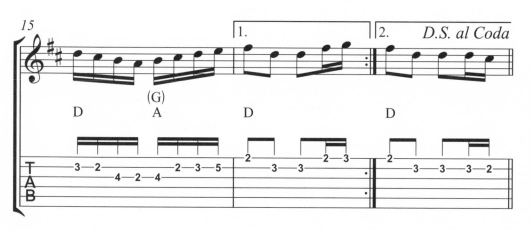

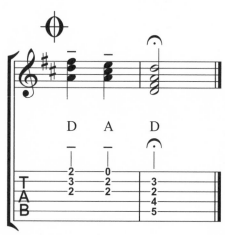

12. Dashing White Sergeant

Trad. arr. Hugh Burns

13. Flirtation

Trad. arr. Hugh Burns

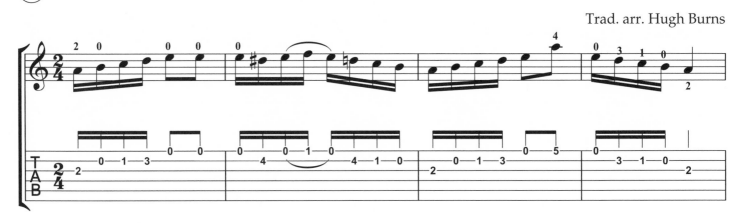

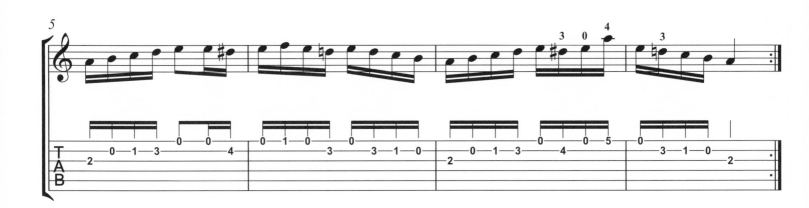

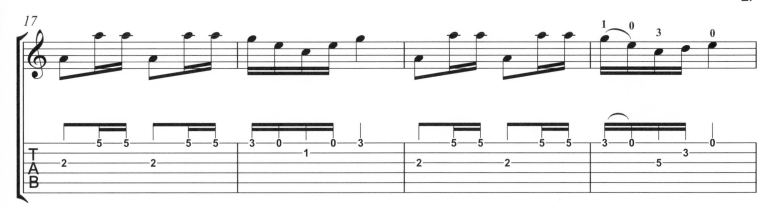

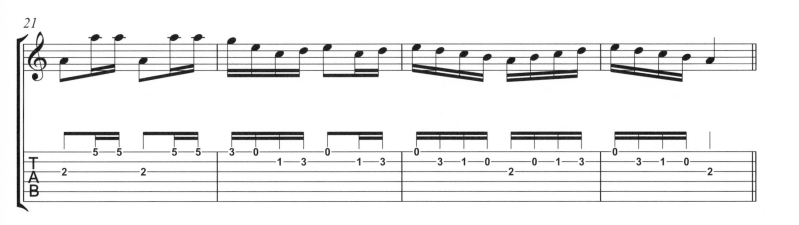

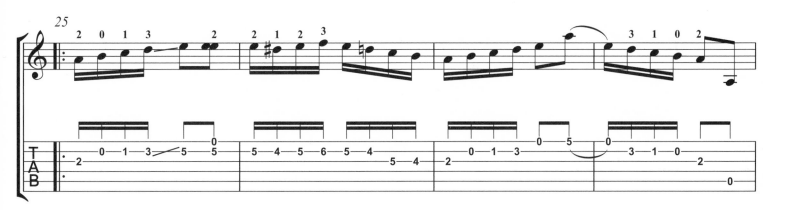

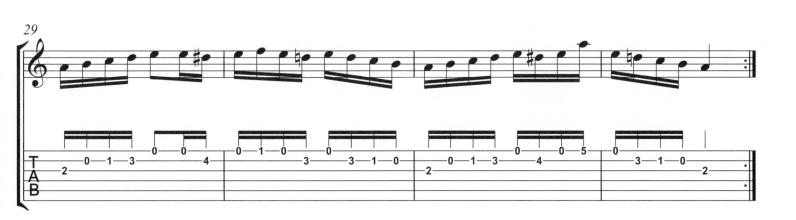

14. Haste to the Wedding

Trad. arr. Hugh Burns

15. Garry Owen

Trad. arr. Hugh Burns

16. Nan Clark's Jig

Hugh Burns

D.C. (with repeats)

repeat last two bars for finish

17. Slip Jig

Hugh Burns

18. Cawdor Fair

Trad. arr. Hugh Burns

© 2011 Schott Music Ltd, London

19. The Keel Row

Trad. arr. Hugh Burns

(repeat from beginning)

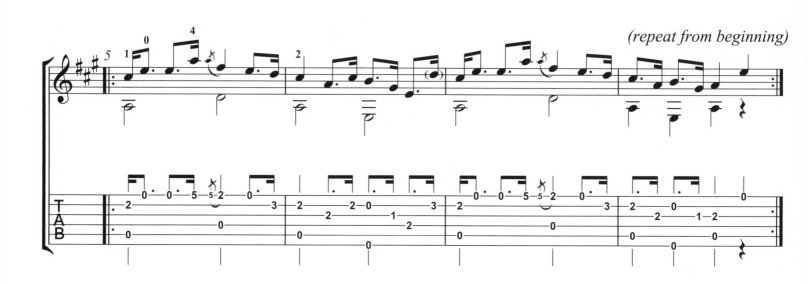

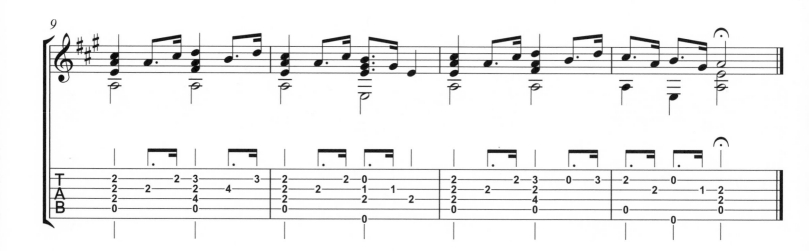

20. Orange and Blue

Trad. arr. Hugh Burns

21. Will Ye Gang to Kelvin Grove

Trad. arr. Hugh Burns

22. A Fond Farewell

(22)

Play with the feeling of a slow air
⑥ = D

Hugh Burns

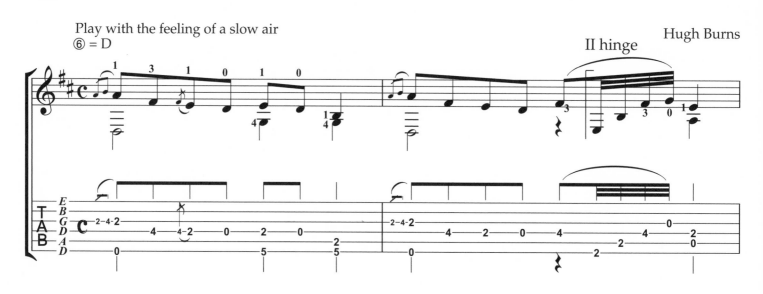

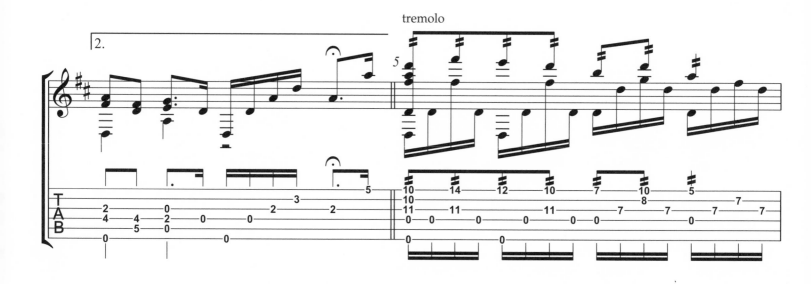

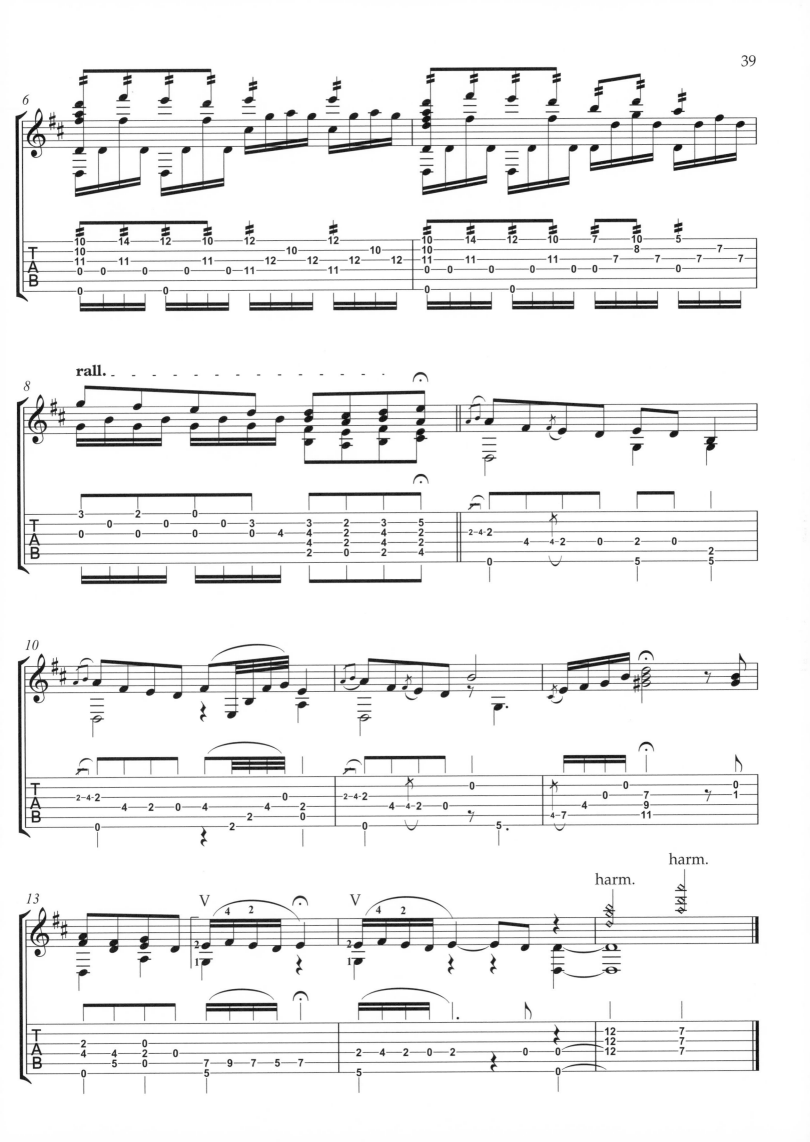

23. The Road and The Miles to Dundee

Capo II
⑥ = D

Trad. arr. Hugh Burns

24. Highland Whiskey

Niel Gow arr. Hugh Burns

play bass on repeat

25. The Braes o' Mar

Trad. arr. Hugh Burns

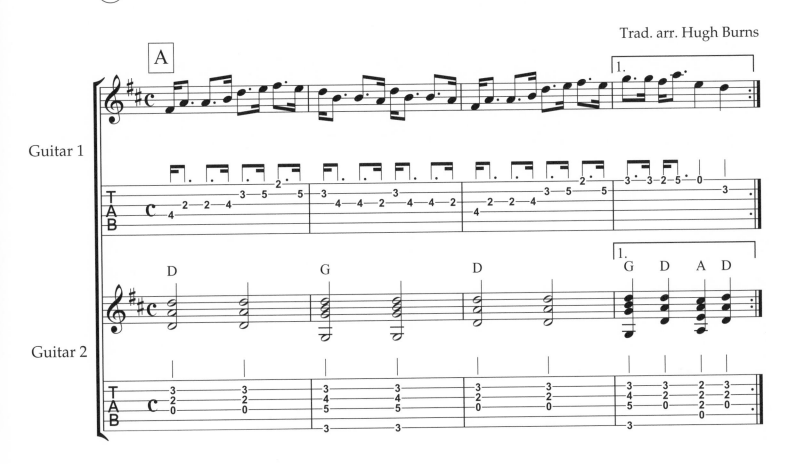

Guitar 1

Guitar 2

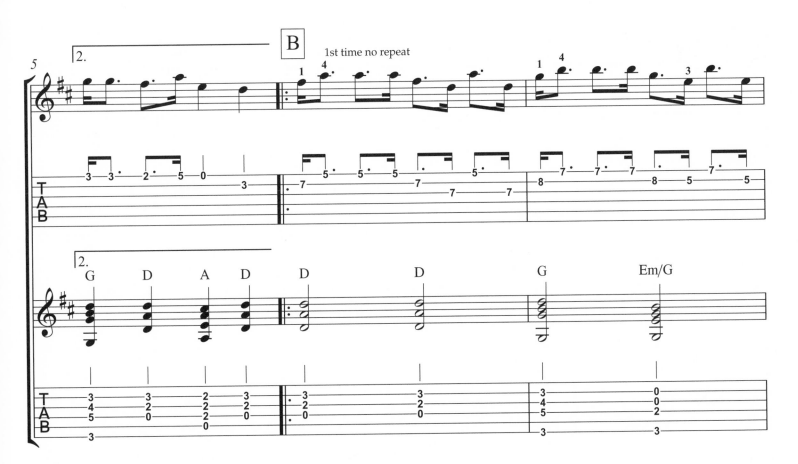

44

Form:

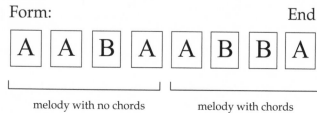

26. The Warrior of Persie

Trad. arr. Hugh Burns

⑥ = D

46

(27)

27. Lewis Wedding Song

Guitar Hi Strung
⑥= D

Lewis arr. Hugh Burns

28. The Rowan Tree

Trad. arr. Hugh Burns

29. Ye Banks and Braes

(Traditional Arrangement)

Trad. arr. Hugh Burns

30. Ye Banks and Braes

Sounds 1 octave higher

Hi Strung

⑥ = D

Trad. arr. Hugh Burns

D.S. al Coda

gradual rall.

31. Saturday Night at The Ceilidh Place

Capo on 2nd fret
⑥ = D

Hugh Burns

D.C. al Coda
(with repeats)

Notes on Tunes

The De'il Among the Tailors
Try to let the notes ring on when possible. This will help to create a harp-like sound. Notice that bars 13, 14, 15 and 16 can be played in the 5th position. The idea of changing the left hand-fingering on the repeat will add interest to the tune.

The Soldier's Joy
This is a classic Reel often played in Scottish, Irish and country sessions. Try to keep the right-hand picking clean. Experiment with alternate up and down picking and for different articulation try a combination of cross and alternate picking. On this recording I used a nylon string guitar.

The Mason's Apron
This is a Reel often played by Scottish country-dance bands. It can be part of a 'set' with 'The De'il Among the Tailors' and 'The Soldier's Joy'. The piece is played finger-style. Pay special attention to the hammer-on and pull-off sections as this technique helps to create a smooth *legato* sound.

The Merry Blacksmith
This popular Reel is played in sessions in the Scottish and Irish traditions. It is a great workout for the right and left hands. Experiment with a combination of alternate picking and hammering-on to achieve a smooth melodic line.

Mrs MacLeod
One of the best-known Scottish Reels. Keep your picking clear and even, take care with the triplet rhythm in bars 17, 19 and 21 in the B section as this is an important feature of contemporary solo playing. There are many versions of this classic Reel with slight variations to the melody. The original is attributed to the great 18th century fiddler Niel Gow. It is even played in the Appalachians under a different title 'Hop High Ladies'!

The Piper o' Dundee
In this solo guitar version of the tune I have written the rhythm slightly simpler than the standard version. This should allow you to focus on the flow and spirit of the piece. The tune is also performed as a vocal piece as there is a very nice lyric to the song.

Logie o' Buchan
This beautiful melody is played in an open 'G' tuning. This brings a special quality to the harmony. The second time through the piece you can add the optional low notes. Also experiment with vibrato and slides, as this will help you to create your own version of the piece.

The Bonnie Lass o' Bon Accord
In this slow air, try to let every note ring out. This will help capture the atmosphere of this beautiful melody. I have included some fingering possibilities, which will help you achieve this.

The Spinning Wheel
Is in the key of F♯ minor. The melody is played in a very plaintive and simple way to bring the best out of it. This beautiful melody looks simple on the page. The difficult part is to sustain the notes and let them ring into each other, hold down the chord shapes and pause after each melodic phrase. I also use open and closed strings to create a 'harp' like effect. Bars 4 and 6 are good example of this style.

MacPherson's Lament
I am playing this version in a G position with the capo at the 2nd fret. It's said that the piece was composed on the eve of MacPherson's execution. I first recorded this tune many years ago for a video about a golf tournament held at the Turnberry course on the west coast of Scotland!

My Love She's But A Lassie Yet
A great one for a Reel set. Take the phrase in bar 7 and use it to develop your alternate picking. Start by setting the metronome at 75bpm, and when that tempo feels comfortable increase it by 5bpm up to 130bpm. Playing a phrase like this as a continuous loop is the best way to sort out any right-hand picking problems. For the singers out there you may want to know that this song has a great lyric written by Robert Burns.

Dashing White Sergeant
This rousing Reel is guaranteed to get the dancers on the floor. A great favourite with many of the classic country dance bands and a great workout for the right hand.

Flirtation
This is a solo piece played with a pick. Keep it moving forward and experiment with different rhythmic values from bar 9 on the octave A notes.

Haste to the Wedding
I have added a rhythm on a second guitar by tapping the body of the instrument. This emulates the sound of the Bodhran. This is a good thing to develop, as it will help your timing. Play this melody with a real 'lilt'.

Garry Owen
This elegant Jig is taken at a medium tempo. Play it at least three times through and as you repeat it, try adding different ornaments.

Nan Clark's Jig
This original finger-style piece needs good right-hand independence to bring out the rhythm of the melody and a clear bass part. The ornaments to the melody can be introduced when you are comfortable with the basic tune.

The first performance of this piece was at the wonderful Ullapool Guitar Festival.

Slip Jig
There is such a strong connection between the Scots and Irish traditions that I have taken a bit of 'artistic licence' to include this original 'Slip Jig'.

In this piece I am tapping the body of the guitar to create a percussive element, which can really add to the music when two or more guitarists are playing together.

Cawdor Fair
This old Scottish tune is known by at least six other titles. It first appears in the Bodleian manuscript under the title 'Cock o' Bendy' and is also known as 'The Hawthorn Tree of Cawdor'. You might also recognise it as a well-known nursery rhyme! Cawdor Castle is said to have a link with the William Shakespeare play Macbeth. However, the 5th Earl of Cawdor said, "I wish the Bard had never written his damned play!"

The Keel Row
Many of the 'Keel Men' of Tyneside were said to have travelled there from the borders of Scotland. There is certainly strong Scottish rhythmic figure in this melody and the tune it is often played for a Strathspey. This version is very straightforward. Try keeping the rhythm of the melody as clear as possible and pay careful attention to the balance between the bass and treble.

Orange and Blue
This is a great introduction to the Scottish snap rhythm used in the Schottische and Strathspey. Keep the picking strong and clear. Note the descending thirds in bars 7 and 15. This is a common melodic device in Scottish dance music.

Will Ye Gang to Kelvin Grove
The song was written by Thomas Lyle (1792–1859) and appeared in his collected poems and songs (1837). The melody was printed in the second volume of the 'Scottish Minstrel' (1811) under the title 'Kelvin Water'.

A Fond Farewell
In this melodic slow air I feature the middle register of the guitar for the verse section. This creates a nice contrast with the melody of the bridge, which is played in the higher octave. The right-hand fingering for the *tremolo* in the bridge is *a m i*.

The Road and the Miles to Dundee
This wonderful traditional song was performed many times at social gatherings when I was a boy. In this simple finger-style arrangement, try to bring out the melody from the chords. One way of doing this is to play the melody with a rest stroke.

Highland Whiskey
Written by one of the greatest Scottish fiddlers of his time, Niel Gow. Born near Dunkeld in 1727, his compositions and arrangements collected by his son Nathaniel have become a rich source for anyone interested in Scottish music.

The Braes o' Mar
An early example of this piece is found in Robert Bremner's Reels (1758). The tune commemorates the raising of the Stuart standard by the 6th Earl of Mar at Braemar. There are a number of different ways of interpreting this tune. This version will give you the basic melody to build your own variations. The melody is played unaccompanied; keep a clear distinction between the Scottish snap rhythm and the dotted quaver rhythm. I introduced some substitute chords on the repeats.

The Warrior of Persie
This slow air has a special atmosphere, and if played slightly faster you can bring out the slow Strathspey rhythm. I have tried to go for almost a free 'Pibroch' feeling. Think of a lone musician playing on a hillside over looking a beautiful loch somewhere in the Scottish Highlands.

Lewis Wedding Song
This is one of the best-known Scottish tunes. In this version I have played the melody the first time through with a simple 'drone' bass. When this section is repeated the bass line descends to give the impression of a 'walking' bass line. Note the triplet ornament on the first phrase of the 'B' section. Note strings 6, 5, 4 and 3 are tuned one octave higher.

The Rowan Tree
Celtic people believe the Rowan Tree could offer protection from evil spirits. Necklaces made with Rowanberries were often worn by highland women to bring luck and ward off evil. In this arrangement I have used DADGAD tuning; notice the slight dissonance in the harmony.

Ye Banks & Braes
This is one of the best-known Scottish traditional songs with words by Robert Burns. There is a version of the melody arranged and published by Niel Gow around 1714. I wanted to show how two completely different arrangements could be achieved with the same simple melody. The first version is similar to the Fernando Sor arrangement using a drop D tuning; the melody is played in 3rds with a simple bass accompaniment. The second version is using a high-strung guitar with a drop D. Strings six, five, four and three are tuned one octave higher than the standard pitch. This is achieved by re-stringing with lighter strings e.g., gauge 34 for sixth, 24 for fifth, 23 for fourth and 11 for third. If the tension is too high for your guitar try lowering the pitch by one whole tone. You

can then capo at the 2nd fret to bring the open string back up to standard concert pitch.

Saturday Night at the Ceilidh Place
I have written the tune as a tribute to the wonderful musical evenings held at the Ceilidh place during the Ullapool Guitar Festival, and a special thanks to all the great guitarists I have had the pleasure of working with in that great venue.

This original piece in DADGAD tuning brings together a number of techniques used in contemporary Celtic guitar playing.

As you play through the tune try some slight variations. I give an example of this on the second repeat of the 'C' section. One way of doing this is to add notes to the chords or slight rhythmic changes to the phrases. This will create interest for the listeners.

Background References
The De'il Among the Tailors, Atholl Collection 1884
Mrs McLeod, Niel Gow's Fifth Collection 1809
MacPherson's rant (lament), Drummond Castle Manuscript 1734
Piper O' Dundee, James Hoggs Jacobite Relics of Scotland 1819
Logie O' Buchan, lyrics in 'Gems of Scottish Song' attributed to George Halket, 1756
The Road and The Miles to Dundee, the first known print copy of the words was in the 'Buchan Observer', 1908
Bonnie Lass o'Bon Accord; Spinning Wheel; Logie o'Buchan; Warrior o'Persie, S.Scott Skinner Collection

Recommended Guitarists
Dick Gaughan, Tony McManus, Clive Carroll, Duck Baker, John Goldie, Davy Graham, John Renbourn, Bert Jansch, Richard Thompson, Martin Carthy, Martin Simpson, Steve Cooney, Tim Edey and Frank Henry

Capo Notation
Capo fret numbering begins from the capo. The capo is used a great deal in traditional music to keep the 'bright' sound of 'open' keys. Remember if you play a 'D' shape with the capo at the 2nd fret the 'concert' key is 'E'.

Notes sur les airs

The De'il Among the Tailors
Essayez de laisser résonner les notes à chaque fois que cela est possible. Cela vous aidera à créer un effet de harpe. Notez que les mesures 13, 14, 15 et 16 peuvent être jouées en 5e position. Un changement de doigté à la main gauche lors de la reprise apportera une touche supplémentaire.

The Soldier's Joy
Il s'agit d'un reel classique souvent joué lors des sessions écossaises, irlandaises et populaires. Essayez de toujours articuler clairement le picking à la main droite. Testez avec le picking alterné haut/bas et pour diversifier l'articulation, vous pouvez tenter une combinaison de cross-picking et de picking alterné.

The Mason's Apron
C'est un reel souvent joué par les groupes de danses folkloriques écossais. Il peut être intégré à un « set » avec De'il Among the Tailors et The Soldier's Joy. Cette pièce se joue aux doigts. Prêtez une attention particulière aux passages hammer-on et pull-off, car cette technique permet de réaliser un legato très doux.

The Merry Blacksmith
Ce reel populaire est joué dans les sessions de tradition écossaise et irlandaise. Il constitue un excellent entraînement pour les deux mains. Testez une combinaison de picking alterné et de hammer-on pour obtenir une ligne mélodique fluide.

Mrs MacLeod
L'un des plus célèbres reels d'Écosse. Conservez un picking clair et régulier, et faites attention aux triolets des mesures 17, 19 et 21 dans la partie B, car ils constituent un élément important du jeu soliste contemporain. Il existe de nombreuses versions de ce reel classique, avec de légères variations mélodiques. La version originale est attribuée à Niel Gow, grand violoniste du 18e siècle. Ce reel est même joué dans les Appalaches, mais sous un titre différent : Hop High Ladies !

The Piper o' Dundee
Dans la présente version de cet air pour guitare seule, j'ai noté le rythme de manière légèrement simplifiée par rapport à la version standard. Cela devrait vous permettre de vous concentrer sur l'esprit et le flux de la pièce. Il en existe également une version vocale sur de très jolies paroles.

Logie o' Buchan
Cette superbe mélodie se joue sur un accord ouvert en sol qui apporte une qualité particulière à l'harmonie. Vous pouvez ajouter les notes graves optionnelles lors la reprise. Testez également le vibrato et les slides, cela vous permettra de créer votre version personnelle de cette pièce.

The Bonnie Lass o' Bon Accord

Essayez de laisser résonner chaque note de ce slow-air. Il vous sera ainsi plus facile de capter l'atmosphère de cette splendide mélodie. J'ai inclus différentes propositions de doigtés qui vous aideront à y parvenir.

The Spinning Wheel

Écrite en *fa*♯ mineur, cette mélodie révèle tout son charme lorsqu'elle est jouée avec simplicité, sur un ton très mélancolique. Cette splendide mélodie semble facile sur le papier. Mais la difficulté est de soutenir les notes et de les laisser résonner l'une dans l'autre, pour y parvenir, tenez les accords et faites une pause après chaque phrase mélodique. J'utilise également les cordes, qu'elles soient à vide ou non, pour créer un effet de « harpe ». Les mesures 4 et 6 sont de bons exemples de ce style.

MacPherson's Lament

Je joue cette version en position de *sol* avec un capodastre sur la deuxième frette. On dit que cette pièce a été composée le soir de l'exécution de MacPherson (célèbre bandit écossais, NDT). Je l'ai enregistrée pour la première fois il y a de nombreuses années pour une vidéo consacrée à un tournoi de golf qui avait lieu sur les parcours de Turnberry, sur la côte ouest de l'Écosse !

My Love She's But a Lassie Yet

Un morceau de choix pour un set de reel. Prenez la phrase de la mesure 7 et utilisez-la pour développer votre picking alterné. Commencez en mettant le métronome à 75 ppm (pulsations par minute), puis, lorsque ce tempo vous semble confortable, augmentez de 5 en 5 jusqu'à 130 ppm. Jouer une phrase comme celle-ci en boucle est la meilleure façon de détecter tout problème de picking à la main droite. Pour les chanteurs, vous serez peut-être intéressés de savoir que cet air possède des paroles magnifiques écrites par Robert Burns.

Dashing White Sergeant

Ce reel exaltant attirera à coup sûr les danseurs sur la piste ! C'est un grand favori de nombreux ensembles de danse folklorique classique qui constitue aussi un excellent entraînement pour la main droite.

Flirtation

Pièce pour guitare seule jouée au médiator. Pensez à toujours aller de l'avant et testez différentes valeurs rythmiques dans la partie B, sur les octaves de *la*.

Haste to the Wedding

J'ai ajouté un rythme frappé sur le corps d'une seconde guitare, imitant ainsi le son du *bodhran*. Jouez cette mélodie avec beaucoup d'entrain.

Garry Owen

Cette jig élégante doit être prise à un tempo moyen.

Jouez-la au moins trois fois et lorsque vous la répétez, tentez de l'embellir par des ornements différents.

Nan Clark Jig

Cette pièce originale à jouer avec les doigts requiert une bonne indépendance de la main droite pour réaliser le rythme de la mélodie et une partie de basse claire. Les ornements de la mélodie pourront être introduits lorsque vous serez à l'aise avec la mélodie de base. Cette pièce a été jouée pour la première fois lors du merveilleux festival de guitare d'Ullapool.

Slip Jig

Les traditions écossaise et irlandaise ont tellement de points communs que je me suis autorisé une petite « licence artistique » en incluant cette slip-jig originale. Dans cette pièce, je frappe de corps de la guitare pour créer un élément percussif qui peut réellement enrichir la musique lorsqu'elle est jouée par deux guitaristes ou davantage.

Cawdor Fair

Ce vieil air écossais est connu sous six titres différents au moins. Il apparaît pour la première fois dans un manuscrit bodléien sous le titre de *Cock o' Bendy* et est également connu sous le titre de *The Hawthorn Tree of Cawdor*. Vous y reconnaîtrez peut-être aussi une célèbre berceuse ! Il semble que le château de Cawdor ait un lien avec *Macbeth*, la pièce de William Shakespeare. Cependant, le cinquième comte de Cawdor aurait dit un jour : « Je voudrais que le barde n'ai jamais écrit cette maudite pièce ! »

The Keel Row

De nombreux pêcheurs de la région de la Tyne, les « Keel Men », sont supposés être arrivés des frontières de l'Écosse. Il est certain que cette mélodie présente des figures rythmiques au caractère typiquement écossais et elle est souvent jouée sous forme de strathspey. La version présentée ici est très simple. Essayez de garder le rythme de la mélodie aussi clair que possible et faites très attention à l'équilibre entre les graves et les aigus.

Orange and Blue

Voici une excellente introduction au *snap rhythm* écossais utilisé dans les écossaises et le strathspey. Veillez à ce que votre picking reste puissant et clair. Notez les tierces descendantes aux mesures 7 et 15. Il s'agit d'un élément mélodique courant dans la musique de danse d'Écosse.

Will Ye Gang to Kelvin Grove

Cet air a été écrit par Thomas Lyle (1792–1859) et apparaît dans son recueil de poèmes et de chansons en 1837. Il a été imprimé dans le second volume du *Scottish Minstrel* sous le titre de *Kelvin Water* en 1881.

A Fond Farewell

Dans le couplet de ce slow-air mélodieux, je mets en avant le registre intermédiaire de la guitare et crée ainsi un contraste intéressant avec la mélodie de transition qui est à l'octave supérieure. Le doigté de la main droite pour le tremolo de la transition est *a m i*.

The Road and the Miles to Dundee

Cet air traditionnel merveilleux était souvent joué lors de réunions entre amis lorsque j'étais enfant. Dans le présent arrangement simple à jouer avec les doigts, veillez à extraire la mélodie des accords. Une façon d'y parvenir est de jouer la mélodie en utilisant la technique du buté.

Highland Whiskey

Mélodie écrite par Niel Gow, l'un des plus grands violonistes écossais de son temps. Niel Gow est né près de Dunkeld en 1727. Ses compositions et ses arrangements, rassemblés par son fils Nathaniel, sont devenus une riche source d'inspiration pour tous ceux qui s'intéressent à la musique écossaise.

The Braes o' Mar

Un des premiers exemplaires de cette pièce figure dans le recueil de reels de Bremner en 1758. Cet air commémore la défense de la maison Stuart par le 6e Comte de Mar at Braemar. Il peut être interprété de nombreuses manières différentes. La présente version vous donne la mélodie de base sur laquelle vous pouvez créer vos propres variations. La mélodie se joue sans accompagnement. Faites bien la distinction entre le *snap rhythm* écossais et le rythme de croche pointée. J'ai ajouté quelques accords alternatifs pour les reprises.

The Warrior of Persie

Ce slow-air dégage une atmosphère particulière. Si vous le jouez assez rapidement, vous pouvez faire ressortir le rythme lent du strathspey. J'ai essayé de favoriser la sensation d'une sorte de « pibroch » libre. Imaginez un musicien solitaire jouant sur une colline au dessus d'un lac splendide, quelque part dans les hautes terres d'Écosse.

Lewis Wedding Song

C'est l'un des airs écossais les plus connus. Dans cette version, je joue une première fois la mélodie avec une ligne de basse constituée d'un simple bourdon. Lors de la reprise de ce passage, la ligne de basse descend pour donner l'impression d'une « walking bass ». Notez le triolet ornemental dans la première phrase de la partie B.

The Rowan Tree

Les Celtes croyaient que le sorbier protégeait des esprits maléfiques. Les femmes des Highlands portaient souvent des colliers de baies de sorbier en guise de porte-bonheur et pour éloigner le mal. Dans cet arrangement, j'ai utilisé un accordage en DADGAD. Notez la légère dissonance dans l'harmonie.

Ye Banks & Braes

C'est là une des chansons traditionnelles écossaises les plus connues, sur des paroles de Robert Burns. Il existe une version de la mélodie arrangée et publiée par Niel Gow vers 1714. J'ai voulu montrer comment deux arrangements totalement différents pouvaient être réalisés à partir de la même mélodie. La première version est similaire à l'arrangement de Fernando Sor et utilise un accordage en Drop D. La mélodie est jouée en tierces parallèles avec une simple ligne d'accompagnement. La seconde version utilise un accordage Drop D sur une guitare dont les cordes 6, 5, 4 et 3 ont été accordées une octave plus haut que la hauteur normale. Pour y parvenir, il faut remplacer les cordes d'origine par des cordes plus légères, par exemple de calibre 34 pour la 6e corde, 24 pour la 5e, 23 pour la 4e et 11 pour la 3e. Si la tension est trop importante pour votre guitare, essayez de baisser l'accord d'un ton entier. Vous pouvez ensuite utiliser un capodastre pour ramener les codes à vide à la fréquence de concert standard.

Saturday Night at the Ceilidh Place

Cet air de ma composition constitue ma contribution aux merveilleuses soirées musicales du « Ceilidh place » pendant le festival de guitare d'Ullapool, en guise de remerciement à tous les grands guitaristes avec qui j'ai eu le plaisir de travailler en ce lieu exceptionnel.

Cette pièce originale nécessitant un accordage en DADGAD rassemble un certain nombre de techniques utilisées dans la pratique contemporaine de la guitare celtique.

Lorsque vous jouez cette pièce, essayez-vous à quelques légères variations. J'en donne un exemple dans la seconde reprise de la partie C. Ajouter des notes aux accords ou procéder à de petites modifications rythmiques dans les phrases sont des façons d'y parvenir. L'intérêt des auditeurs s'en trouvera accru.

Références
The De'il Among the Tailors, Atholl Collection 1884
Mrs McLeod, Niel Gow's Fifth Collection 1809
MacPherson's rant (lament), Drummond Castle Manuscript 1734
Piper o' Dundee, James Hoggs Jacobite Relics of Scotland 1819
Logie o' Buchan, paroles dans "Gems of Scottish Song" attribué à George Halket, 1756
The Road and The Miles to Dundee, première version imprimée connue des paroles dans le « Buchan Observer » en 1908
Bonnie Lass o'Bon Accord; Spinning Wheel; Logie o'Buchan; Warrior o'Persie, S.Scott Skinner Collection

Interprètes recommandés
Dick Gaughan, Tony McManus, Clive Carroll, Duck Baker, John Goldie, Davy Graham, John Renbourn, Bert Jansch, Richard Thompson, Martin Carthy, Martin Simpson, Steve Cooney, Tim Edey and Frank Henry

Anmerkungen zu den Stücken

The De'il Among the Tailors
Wenn möglich, sollten die Töne nachklingen. Dadurch entsteht ein harfenähnlicher Klang. Takt 13, 14, 15 und 16 können in der 5. Lage gespielt werden. Ein anderer Fingersatz bei der Wiederholung macht Stück interessanter.

The Soldier's Joy
Dieses Stück ist ein klassischer Reel, der oft in schottischen, irischen und Country Sessions gespielt wird. Das Plektrumspiel mit der rechten Hand sollte immer sauber klingen. Du kannst mit dem Alternate Picking experimentieren und als Artikulationsvariante eine Kombination aus Cross- und Alternate Picking ausprobieren.

The Mason's Apron
Dieser Reel wird oft von schottischen Country-Dance-Bands gespielt. Er kann zusammen mit „De'il Among the Tailors" und „The Soldier's Joy" ein „Set" bilden. Das Stück wird gezupft. Beachte insbesondere die Hammer-on- und Pull-off-Passagen, da diese Techniken zu einem gleichmäßigen Legato-Klang beitragen. Für diese Aufnahme habe ich eine Gitarre mit Nylonsaiten verwendet.

The Merry Blacksmith
Dieser beliebte Reel wird in Sessions gemäß den schottischen und irischen Traditionen gespielt. Er ist eine hervorragende Übung für die rechte und linke Hand. Man kann mit einer Kombination aus Alternate Picking und Hammering experimentieren, um eine fließende Melodielinie zu erzeugen.

Mrs MacLeod
Einer der bekanntesten schottischen Reels. Das Picking sollte sauber und gleichmäßig sein. Beachte den Triolenrhythmus in Takt 17, 19 und 21 im B-Teil, da er ein wichtiger Bestandteil des zeitgenössischen Solospiels ist. Es gibt viele Versionen dieses klassischen Reels mit kleinen Variationen in der Melodie. Das Original wird Niel Gow, dem berühmten Fiddler des 18. Jahrhunderts, zugeschrieben. Das Stück wird sogar in den Appalachen gespielt, wenn auch unter einem anderen Titel: „Hop High Ladies".

The Piper o' Dundee
Für diese Sologitarrenversion habe ich den Rhythmus gegenüber der Standardversion etwas vereinfacht. Somit kann man sich besser auf den Ablauf und die Stimmung des Stücks konzentrieren. Das Stück wird auch gesungen, da es einen sehr schönen Text hat.

Logie o' Buchan
Diese schöne Melodie wird in der offenen G-Stimmung gespielt, was den Harmonien eine besondere Qualität verleiht. Bei der Wiederholung kannst du die optionalen tiefen Töne hinzufügen. Darüber hinaus kannst du mit Vibrato und Slides experimentieren und dem Stück somit eine ganz persönliche Note verleihen.

The Bonnie Lass o' Bon Accord
In diesem Slow Air sollte jeder Ton nachklingen, um die Atmosphäre der schönen Melodie eingefangen. Ich habe einige Fingersatzmöglichkeiten angegeben, die dazu beitragen, dass dir dies gelingt.

The Spinning Wheel
Das Stück steht in fis-Moll. Die Melodie wird sehr schwermütig und schlicht gespielt, um sie möglichst gut zur Geltung zu bringen. Die Noten sehen zwar ganz einfach aus, doch ist es recht schwierig, die Töne zu halten und miteinander zu verschmelzen, die Griffe zu halten und nach jeder Melodiephrase innezuhalten. Außerdem verwende ich leere und gegriffene Saiten, um einen harfenartigen Effekt zu erzeugen. Takt 4 und 6 sind gute Beispiele für dieses Stilmittel.

MacPherson's Lament
Ich spiele diese Version in der G-Lage mit dem Capo im 3. Bund. Angeblich wurde das Stück am Abend vor Macphersons Hinrichtung komponiert. Ich habe es vor vielen Jahren zum ersten Mal für ein Video über ein Golfturnier in Turnberry an der Westküste Schottlands aufgenommen.

My Love She's But a Lassie Yet
Ein tolles Stück für ein Reel-Set. Mit der Phrase in Takt 7 kannst du deine Alternate-Picking-Technik verbessern. Am besten stellst du das Metronom zuerst auf 75 bpm ein und erhöhst dann immer um 5 bpm bis auf 130 bpm. Wenn du eine Phrase immer wieder auf diese Weise spielst, kannst du Probleme beim Plektrumspiel mit der rechten Hand rasch beseitigen. Für die Sänger unter euch ist es vielleicht ganz interessant, dass der Song auch einen Text hat, der von Robert Burns stammt.

Dashing White Sergeant
Bei diesem mitreißenden Reel wird die Tanzfläche garantiert voll. Das Stück ist bei vielen klassischen Country-Dance-Bands sehr beliebt und ist eine hervorragende Übung für die rechte Hand.

Flirtation
Dieses Solostück wird mit dem Plektrum gespielt und sollte durchgängig dynamisch klingen. Im B-Teil kannst du mit verschiedenen rhythmischen Werten auf den oktavierten *A*s experimentieren.

Haste To The Wedding
Ich habe einen Rhythmus hinzugefügt, indem ich auf den Korpus einer zweiten Gitarre geklopft habe. Das klingt so

ähnlich wie eine Bodhrán und trägt zur Entwicklung eines guten Taktgefühls bei. Die Melodie sollte richtig „beschwingt" gespielt werden.

Garry Owen
Dieser elegante Jig ist mittelschnell. Er sollte mindestens dreimal komplett gespielt werden, wobei du bei jeder Wiederholung andere Verzierungen ausprobieren kannst.

Nan Clark Jig
Dieses Original-Fingerstyle-Stück erfordert eine ausgeprägte Unabhängigkeit der rechten Hand, um den Rhythmus der Melodie und die Bassstimme zur Geltung zu bringen. Du kannst die Verzierungen in der Melodie auch erst dann hinzufügen, wenn dir das Stück ansonsten keine Probleme mehr bereitet. Das Stück wurde zum ersten Mal beim Gitarrenfestival in Ullapool gespielt.

Slip Jig
Die schottischen und irischen Traditionen sind so eng miteinander verbunden, dass ich mir hier ein wenig „künstlerische Freiheit" erlaubt und diesen Original-„Slip Jig" eingebaut habe.

In diesem Stück klopfe ich auf den Korpus der Gitarre, um ein perkussives Element zu erzeugen und das Stück zu bereichern, wenn zwei oder mehr Gitarristen zusammen spielen.

Cawdor Fair
Dieses alte schottische Stück ist unter mindestens sechs weiteren Titeln bekannt. Es erschien erstmals im Bodleian Manuscript unter dem Titel „Cock o' Bendy" und ist auch als „The Hawthorn Tree of Cawdor" bekannt. Cawdor Castle hat angeblich einen engen Bezug zu dem Shakespeare-Stück „Macbeth". Allerdings sagte der 5. Earl of Cawdor: „Ich wünschte, der Barde hätte das verdammte Stück nie geschrieben!"

The Keel Row
Viele der „Keelmen" in Tyneside kamen angeblich aus den Grenzgebieten Schottlands. Die Melodie enthält eine typisch schottische Rhythmusfigur, und das Stück wird häufig als Strathspey gespielt. Die vorliegende Version ist sehr geradlinig. Der Rhythmus der Melodie sollte so sauber wie möglich gespielt werden. Achte insbesondere auf das Gleichgewicht zwischen Bass und Oberstimme.

Orange and Blue
Dieses Stück ist eine gute Einführung in den Scottish-Snap-Rhythmus, der im Schottisch und Strathspey vorkommt. Das Plektrumspiel sollte kräftig und deutlich sein. Beachte die absteigenden Terzen in Takt 7 und 15. Sie sind ein gängiges melodisches Stilmittel in der schottischen Tanzmusik.

Will Ye Gang to Kelvin Grove
Das Lied wurde von Thomas Lyle (1792–1859) geschrieben und erschien in seinen „Collected Poems and Songs" (1837). Die Melodie wurde unter dem Titel „Kelvin Water" im zweiten Band des „Scottish Minstrel" (1811) veröffentlicht.

A Fond Farewell
In diesem melodischen Slow Air spiele ich die Strophen in der mittleren Lage der Gitarre. Dadurch entsteht ein schöner Kontrast zur Melodie der Bridge, die in der höheren Oktave gespielt wird. Der Fingersatz der rechten Hand für das Tremolo in der Bridge ist *a m i*.

The Road and the Miles to Dundee
Dieses Volkslied wurde sehr oft bei Zusammenkünften gespielt, als ich noch ein Kind war. In dieser einfachen Fingerstyle-Bearbeitung sollte sich die Melodie deutlich von den Akkorden abheben. Zu diesem Zweck kann die Melodie mit der Apoyando-Technik gespielt werden.

Highland Whiskey
Das Stück wurde von einem der berühmtesten schottischen Fiddler jener Zeit geschrieben: Niel Gow, der 1727 in der Nähe von Dunkeld geboren wurde. Seine Kompositionen und Bearbeitungen, die von seinem Sohn Nathaniel gesammelt wurden, sind eine Fundgrube für alle, die sich für schottische Musik interessieren.

The Braes o' Mar
Ein frühes Beispiel dieses Stücks ist in Robert Bremners Reels (1758) zu finden. Das Stück erinnert daran, dass der 6. Earl of Mar in Braemar die Standarte für James Stuart hisste. Es gibt zahlreiche Interpretationsmöglichkeiten für dieses Stück. Die vorliegende Version besteht aus der Grundmelodie, die beliebig variiert werden kann. Die Melodie wird ohne Begleitung gespielt. Der Unterschied zwischen dem Scottish Snap und dem punktierten Achtelrhythmus sollte deutlich zu hören sein. Bei den Wiederholungen habe ich ein paar Stellvertreterakkorde eingeführt.

The Warrior of Persie
Dieses Slow Air hat eine ganz besondere Atmosphäre. Wenn es etwas schneller gespielt wird, kommt der langsame Strathspey-Rhythmus gut zur Geltung. Ich habe versucht, eine Art freies Piobaireachd-Feeling zu erzeugen. Stell dir einen einsamen Musiker vor, der irgendwo in den schottischen Highlands auf einem Hügel mit Blick auf einen wunderschönen See spielt.

Lewis Wedding Song
Dies ist eine der bekanntesten schottischen Melodien. In der vorliegenden Version spiele ich die Melodie das erste Mal mit einem einfachen „Bordunbass". Bei der Wiederholung dieses Teils vermittelt die absteigende

Bassstimme den Eindruck eines „Walking Bass". Beachte die Triolenverzierung in der ersten Phrase des B-Teils. Beachte, dass die 6., 5., 4. und 3. Saite eine Oktave höher gestimmt sind.

The Rowan Tree

Ein keltischer Glaube besagt, dass der Rowan Tree (Vogelbeere) Schutz vor bösen Geistern bietet. Frauen aus den Highlands trugen oft Halsketten aus Vogelbeeren, die Glück bringen und Unheil fernhalten sollten. In dieser Bearbeitung habe ich die DADGAD-Stimmung verwendet. Beachte die leichte Dissonanz in den Akkorden.

Ye Banks & Braes

Dies ist eines der bekanntesten schottischen Volkslieder mit einem Text von Robert Burns. Es gibt eine Version der Melodie, die um 1714 von Niel Gow bearbeitet und veröffentlicht wurde. Ich wollte zeigen, wie zwei völlig unterschiedliche Bearbeitungen aus derselben einfachen Melodie entstehen können. Die erste Version ähnelt der Bearbeitung von Fernando Sor in der Dropped-D-Stimmung. Die Melodie wird in Terzen und mit einer einfachen Bassbegleitung gespielt. Die zweite Version wird auf einer hoch gestimmten Gitarre mit dropped D gespielt. Die sechste, fünfte, vierte und dritte Saite werden eine Oktave höher gestimmt. Dazu braucht man dünnere Saiten, z.B. in der Stärke .034 für die sechste Saite, .024 für die fünfte, .023 für die vierte und .011 für die dritte. Wenn die Spannung für deine Gitarre zu hoch ist, kannst du versuchen, sie um einen Ganzton herunterzustimmen. Anschließend spielst du mit dem Kapodaster im 2. Bund, um die Leersaite wieder nach oben zur Standardstimmung zu bringen.

Saturday Night at the Ceilidh Place

Ich habe das Stück als Erinnerung an die herrlichen Musikabende im Ceilidh Place während des Ullapool-Gitarrenfestivals geschrieben und danke hiermit allen Gitarristen, mit denen ich dort arbeiten durfte.

Das Original in der DADGAD-Stimmung vereint eine Reihe von Techniken, die heute in der keltischen Gitarrenmusik eingesetzt werden.

Du kannst beim Spielen dieses Stücks ein paar kleine Variationen ausprobieren. Ich gebe bei der zweiten Wiederholung des C-Teils ein Beispiel dafür. Du kannst z.B. zusätzliche Akkordtöne spielen oder den Rhythmus der Phrasen leicht verändern. Das klingt dann für die Zuhörer interessanter.

Quellenangaben
The De'il Among the Tailors, *Atholl Collection*, 1884
Mrs McLeod, Niel Gows *Fifth Collection*, 1809
MacPherson's Rant (Lament), *Drummond Castle Manuscript*, 1734
Piper o' Dundee, James Hoggs *Jacobite Relics of Scotland*, 1819
Logie o' Buchan, Text in „Gems of Scottish Song", vermutlich von George Halket (1756)
The Road and The Miles to Dundee, erster bekannte Abdruck des Textes im „Buchan Observer", 1908

Bonnie Lass o'Bon Accord; Spinning Wheel; Logie o'Buchan; Warrior o'Persie, S.Scott Skinner Collection

Empfohlene Gitarristen
Dick Gaughan, Tony McManus, Clive Carroll, Duck Baker, John Goldie, Davy Graham, John Renbourn, Bert Jansch, Richard Thompson, Martin Carthy, Martin Simpson, Steve Cooney, Tim Edey and Frank Henry

Capo-Notation
Die Nummerierung der Bünde beginnt am Capo. Der Capo wird in der traditionellen Musik häufig eingesetzt, um den „klaren" Klang der „offenen" Akkorde beizubehalten. Beachte, dass ein D-Akkord mit dem Capo im 2. Bund wie ein E-Akkord klingt.

Further Guitar Titles Available from Schott Music

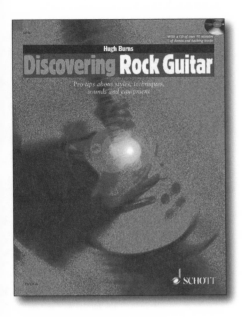

Discovering Rock Guitar
ED 12946

SCHOTT POP STYLES

Discovering Rock Guitar
by Hugh Burns

An introduction to rock and pop styles, techniques, sounds and equipment

- Learn insider secrets of rock guitar playing from top session guitarist Hugh Burns

- Focusing on 15 key rock styles from the 1950s to the present day

- Get the low-down on gear, amps and guitars used on classic rock arrangements

- The accompanying CD includes complete demonstrations of 15 sample tracks, recorded by Hugh Burns, together with backing tracks to play along with

---

Romantic Guitar Anthology

Original Works and Transcriptions from the Romantic period selected and edited by Jens Franke

- Both mainstream and lesser-known works from composers such as Berlioz, Paganini, Mertz, Schubert and Schumann

- Graded pieces new to the graded framework presented in a progressive order

- Extensive commentary on each piece

- Composer biographies included

- CD recording of all the pieces played by Jens Franke

Volume 1	(Grades 1-2)	ED 13110
Volume 2	(Grades 3-4)	ED 13111
Volume 3	(Grades 5-6)	ED 13112
Volume 4	(Grades 7-8)	ED 13113

CD Track List / Plages du CD / CD-Titelverzeichnis

1.	The De'il Among the Tailors (Reel)	1:11
2.	The Soldier's Joy (Reel)	1:47
3.	The Mason's Apron (Reel)	1:22
4.	The Merry Blacksmith (Reel)	0:46
5.	Mrs MacLeod (Reel)	1:34
6.	The Piper o' Dundee (Jig)	1:03
7.	Logie o'Buchan (Slow Air)	1:10
8.	The Bonnie Lass of Bon Accord (Slow Air)	3:09
9.	The Spinning Wheel (Slow Air)	1:45
10.	MacPherson's Lament (Slow Sir)	1:29
11.	My Love She's But a Lassie (Petronella)	1:09
12.	Dashing White Sergeant (Petronella)	0:57
13.	Flirtation	1:07
14.	Haste to the Wedding (Jig)	1:08
15.	Garry Owen (Jig)	0:44
16.	Nan Clark's Jig	1:06
17.	Slip Jig	0:55
18.	Cawdor Fair (Strathspey)	0:52
19.	The Keel Row (Strathspey)	1:00
20.	Orange and Blue (Strathspey)	0:57
21.	Will Ye Gang to Kelvin Grove (Waltz)	1:18
22.	A Fond Farewell (Slow Air)	2:02
23.	The Road and the Miles to Dundee (Slow Air)	1:58
24.	Highland Whiskey (Strathspey)	1:00
25.	The Braes o'Mar (Strathspey)	1:12
26.	The Warrior of Persie (Slow Air)	1:30
27.	Lewis Wedding Song	1:00
28.	The Rowan Tree (Waltz)	1:50
29.	Ye Banks and Braes (Traditional Arrangement)	1:34
30.	Ye Banks and Braes	2:17
31.	Saturday Night at the Ceilidh Place	1:46
		Total: 42:38